Marvelous Miso Recipes

An Illustrated Cookbook of Super Asian Dish Ideas!

BY: ROSE RIVERA

© 2022 Rose Rivera All Rights Reserved

A Book Copyright Page

All rights are reserved for this book. On no account you are allowed to copy, print, publish, sell or make any kind of change to this book. Only the author has this permission. In case you have a copied version of this book please delete it and get the original one. It will support the author and he will be able to make even more helpful and fun cookbooks.

Make sure that you take every step with caution when you follow the instruction in this book. It's a book with information that was doubled checked by the author but you are responsible for your own actions and decisions.

Table of Contents

Introduction

How can miso add authentic Asian flavor to your everyday recipes?

Are you interested in adding a unique taste to otherwise bland dishes?

Are the ingredients found in your local area, or can you order them online?

You can enjoy miso, either raw or cooked, in many dishes. Add it just before you finish cooking your favorite recipes. Don't boil miso soup or other dishes, or the heat can kill off its beneficial active bacteria.

When you buy pre-made miso, it's ready to be used from the container. It will add the saltiness of umami to all kinds of dishes. It's found in Asian groceries & health food stores.

Miso can range from dark brown to pale tan or reddish-brown. Its flavor varies with the colors. As a rule, miso tends to be savory, salty, and tangy. The lighter types are usually a bit sweeter. It isn't meant to be consumed alone but rather used to enhance the flavor of dishes you're preparing. Miso is excellent in soups based around it, but it also adds savory, rich flavor to many dishes without overpowering them. Read on and learn more about miso…

1 – Grilled Miso Bok Choy

This is one of our favorite summer side dishes. It's quite a tasty vegetable, and after it's sauced and grilled, it's wonderful.

Makes 4 Servings

Cooking + Prep Time: 20 minutes

Ingredients:

- 4 bok choy, baby
- 1 tbsp of oil, olive
- 1 tbsp of soy sauce, reduced-sodium
- 1 tbsp of miso paste
- 1/4 tsp of salt, kosher

Instructions:

Preheat your grill for med-high heat.

Slice bok choy in halves.

In a large bowl, whisk together the miso paste, soy sauce, oil, and salt. Add bok choy. Toss till coated fully.

Place bok choy on grill grates. Grill till tender, 3-4 minutes on each side. Serve.

2 – Tomatoes & Eggplant with Miso-Ginger Dressing

The tomatoes are the base of this recipe, and keeping a well-oiled, clean grill grate will make them perfect. The miso-ginger dressing is SO addictive.

Makes 4 Servings

Cooking + Prep Time: 35 minutes

Ingredients:

- 1 x 1" piece of peeled and sliced ginger, fresh
- 1/4 cup of miso, white (soybean paste, fermented)
- 1 tbsp of vinegar, rice
- 1 tbsp of toasted sesame seeds
- 3 tbsp of oil, vegetable
- 1 x 1" wedge-cut eggplant
- 4 lengthwise-halved plum tomatoes, ripe and firm
- Salt, kosher & pepper, ground, as desired

Instructions:

Blend the 1 tbsp of oil, sesame seeds, vinegar, miso, and ginger in a food processor. Add the water 1 teaspoon until you have a creamy mixture. Set this dressing aside.

Prepare your grill for med-high heat. Use the last 2 tbsp of oil to rub over tomatoes and eggplant. Season them with kosher salt & ground pepper, as desired. Grill for 4 to 6 minutes on each side, till tender and charred. Serve them with the miso-ginger dressing.

3 – Tofu Miso Stir Fry

Not a tofu fan yet? You just might be, after you enjoy this stir fry. The miso-based sauce makes it unique and seasoned perfectly.

Makes 4 Servings

Cooking + Prep Time: 35 minutes

Ingredients:

For sauce:

- 1/4 cup of soy sauce, reduced-sodium
- 6 tbsp of water, filtered
- 1 tbsp of vinegar, rice
- 2 tbsp of sugar, granulated
- 1 tbsp of miso paste, white or yellow
- 1/4 tsp of garlic powder
- 2 tsp of corn starch

For stir fry:

- 6 heaping cups of broccoli florets
- 1 bell pepper, red
- Optional: 4 oz. of mushrooms, shiitake
- 2 onions, green
- 1 tbsp of grated ginger, fresh
- 14 oz. of tofu, firm/extra firm
- 3 tbsp of oil, sesame
- Salt, kosher, as desired
- For garnishing: Sesame seeds, as desired

Instructions:

To prepare sauce, whisk ingredients for the sauce in a medium-sized bowl.

Chop broccoli into florets if not already done. Slice pepper thinly. Remove stems of shiitake mushrooms, then slice them thinly. Slice green onion thinly. Peel, then grate the ginger.

Cut tofu into small pieces. Pat dry using a clean towel. Add 2 tbsp of sesame oil to a large pan. Add tofu cubes & several pinches of salt. Set heat on med-high. Cook tofu till bottom is browned lightly, 5-6 minutes.

Remove pan briefly from heat. Flip tofu pieces. Return pan to med-high heat. Cook till browned, 5-6 minutes. Remove tofu to a bowl. Set bowl aside.

Add the last tbsp of oil to the skillet. Add peppers, broccoli & mushrooms. Add 2 pinches of salt. Stir occasionally till edges start to brown, 6-7 minutes. During the last minute of cooking, add a tbsp of filtered water. Let vegetable steam.

Reduce heat to a low level. Add ginger and green onion and cook for a minute. Turn off heat. Add sauce and tofu. Stir till sauce has thickened. Use sesame seeds to garnish, as desired. Serve promptly.

4 – Miso - Garlic Green Beans

The beans in this dish are amazingly flavorful, especially if you give them time to blister and char. The garlic and miso add such a unique flavor.

Makes 6 Servings

Cooking + Prep Time: 30 minutes

Ingredients:

- 3 finely chopped cloves of garlic
- 3 tbsp of lime juice, fresh
- 3 tbsp of miso, white
- 1 tbsp of agave or coconut nectar
- 3 tbsp of coconut oil, virgin
- 1 & 1/2 lbs. of trimmed green beans
- A pinch of crushed pepper flakes, red
- Sea salt, flaky, as desired
- Pepper, ground, as desired
- 1/3 cup of cilantro, chopped coarsely

Instructions:

Mix the lime juice, garlic, nectar, and miso in a small bowl and combine well. Set mixture aside.

Heat the oil in a skillet on med-high heat. Add the green beans. Cook them without stirring for 2-3 minutes, till they start blistering. Then toss them and continue tossing as you cook them for 8 to 12 minutes, till tender and with blisters here and there.

Remove the skillet from heat. Then pour in the garlic mixture. Toss till the green beans are coated. Add the pepper flakes. Season using sea salt & ground pepper, as desired. Transfer beans to a serving platter. Top them with cilantro and serve.

5 – Miso Soba Noodles

Are you hungry for noodles but don't want to take a long time to prepare them? These soba noodles, so simple and fast, are filled with flavor.

Makes 4 Servings

Cooking + Prep Time: 15 minutes

Ingredients:

- 8 oz. of noodles, soba
- 1/4 cup of soy sauce, reduced-sodium
- 3 tbsp of sesame oil, toasted
- 2 tbsp of vinegar, rice
- 1 tbsp of maple syrup or honey
- Optional: 1 tbsp of miso
- 1 tsp of garlic, grated
- 4 onions, green
- Optional: Sriracha sauce, as desired
- Sesame seeds, toasted, as desired for garnishing

Instructions:

Cook noodles using directions on the package.

Whisk soy sauce, sesame oil, vinegar, syrup or honey, miso & garlic in a medium-sized bowl.

Diagonally slice green onions thinly. Use dark green and white parts.

Return soba noodles to the pan. Stir in green onions and sauce. If desired, add to individual bowls and top them with the sesame seeds. Serve.

6 – Clam Chowder with Miso

Clam chowder has been a popular comfort food for many years. When you add miso, it gives the soup more depth of body and flavor. It's always a hit in our home in the wintertime.

Makes 4 Servings

Cooking + Prep Time: 1 hour & 5 minutes

Ingredients:

- 1 tbsp of butter, unsalted
- 3 oz. of chopped pancetta
- 1/2 cup of chopped onion
- 2 chopped cloves of garlic
- 1 thyme sprig, fresh
- 1 cup of dry wine, white
- 1 lb. of peeled, cubed russet potatoes
- 2 cups of chicken broth, low-salt
- 2 tbsp of miso
- 1 cup of cream, heavy
- 12 littleneck clams, scrubbed
- Tabasco sauce, as desired
- Chopped parsley, flat-leaf, as desired

Instructions:

Melt the butter in a large pan on med heat. Add the pancetta. Cook for 5 to 6 minutes, till rendered slightly.

Add thyme, onions, and garlic. Stir often while cooking for 4 to 5 minutes, till onions have softened. Add the wine and bring the mixture to a boil. Reduce the heat and allow to simmer for 2 to 3 minutes. Add miso, cream, broth, and potatoes. Simmer for 20 to 30 minutes, till potatoes have become tender.

Add the clams. Cover the pan and cook for 5 to 7 minutes, till the clams have opened. Season with tabasco sauce to taste and use parsley as desired for garnish. Serve.

7 – Miso Cauliflower Stir-Fry

This is my favorite way to enjoy cauliflower. It's fried till tender and lightly charred, then mixed with peppers and a tasty sauce. Even children love this recipe!

Makes 3-4 Servings

Cooking + Prep Time: 25 minutes

Ingredients:

- 1 x 2-lb. head of cauliflower
- 1 each bell pepper, red & orange
- 1 white onion, medium
- 3 onions, green
- 3 tbsp of vinegar, rice
- 2 pinches of salt, kosher
- 1/4 cup of soy sauce, reduced-sodium
- 1 tbsp of miso, light
- 2 tbsp of maple syrup or granulated sugar
- 2 tbsp of untoasted sesame oil
- 1 tsp of corn starch
- 3 tbsp of oil, canola or olive

Instructions:

Chop cauliflower head in small-sized florets. Slice bell peppers, green onion, and white onion thinly.

In a medium-sized bowl, whisk vinegar, miso, soy sauce, sesame oil, sugar/syrup & corn starch together.

In a large, non-stick skillet, heat 2 tbsp oil on med-high. Add cauliflower & a pinch of kosher salt. Cook without stirring till the cauliflower is charred, 3-4 minutes. Flip florets and cook for 2 more minutes.

Add the last tbsp of oil, along with another pinch of kosher salt, white onions, and bell peppers. Cook till tender, 4-6 minutes.

Turn heat off. Pour in sauce & add green onions. Then stir till sauce has thickened and coated all veggies. Serve promptly.

8 – Chicken Kombu Miso Soup

This simple soup has a dashi base, which brings out its flavors. The same stock is also a base for miso soup, and this option is possibly at its most delicious if you make it with chicken stock.

Makes 4 Servings

Cooking + Prep Time: 45 minutes

Ingredients:

- 1/4 cup of water, filtered
- 1 bunch of trimmed spinach
- 3 x 4"x6" pieces of kombu, dried – available in Asian markets
- 1 cup of bonito flakes
- 6 cups of chicken stock, low-sodium
- 2 tbsp of soy sauce, reduced-sodium
- 2 tbsp of mirin
- Salt, kosher, as desired
- 2 lengthwise-halved, thinly crosswise-sliced chicken breasts, skinless, boneless
- 1 peeled, 2"-matchstick cut carrot, medium
- 4 oz. of thinly-sliced, stemmed mushrooms, shiitake
- To serve: sesame seeds, toasted, as desired

Instructions:

Add 1/4 cup of filtered water to a large skillet on med heat and heat it. Once it steams, add the spinach. Toss often while cooking for 2 minutes, till spinach starts wilting. Transfer to a colander and allow spinach to cool. Squeeze to get rid of any excess water. Chop spinach coarsely and set it aside.

Bring the stock and kombu to simmer in a large pan on low heat. Then remove the pan from the heat & allow it to set for 8-10 minutes. Return to simmer, then add the bonito flakes. Remove from the heat and allow to sit for 2-3 minutes. Strain the kombu mixture through a sieve into a large-sized bowl.

Wipe out saucepan. Return the broth to that pan. Add soy sauce and mirin. Season with kosher salt, as desired. Bring to simmer on med heat. Add chicken, mushrooms, and carrots. Cook till chicken has cooked fully through with no pink remaining. Carrots and mushrooms should cook for 4 to 6 minutes, till barely tender.

Divide the spinach into bowls. Ladle soup on top. Sprinkle over with sesame seeds, if desired, and serve.

9 – Miso Shrimp Bisque

This bisque is fancy enough for special occasions. You can also prepare it any weeknight and freeze 1/2 of it for another day.

Makes 8 Servings

Cooking + Prep Time: 1 & 3/4 hour

Ingredients:

- 1 pound shrimps, in-shell
- 2 tbsp of oil, canola
- 6 tbsp of tomato paste, no salt added
- 2 cups of roughly chopped onions
- 1 cup of roughly chopped carrots
- 1 cup of roughly chopped celery
- 6 cups of water, filtered
- 1 bay leaf, medium
- 4 cups of chicken stock, low sodium
- 1/2 cup of rice, Basmati
- 5 tbsp of miso, red
- 1/4 cup of sherry, cooking or dry
- 1 tbsp of oil, olive
- 1/2 tsp of soup seasoning, salt-free

Instructions:

Peel the shrimp and devein them. You can leave the tails on or remove them. Place shrimp in the refrigerator and reserve the shells.

Heat the oil in a large pot on med heat. Add the shrimp shells. Stir constantly while cooking for 3 to 4 minutes, till they turn bright red.

Add the celery, tomato paste, onions, and carrots. Stir constantly for 3 more minutes, till the mixture is fragrant. Add bay leaf and 6 cups of filtered water. Increase the heat level to high.

Bring mixture to boil. Cover pot. Reduce the heat level to low and simmer for 45 to 55 minutes. Pour through a fine strainer into a large-sized bowl. Discard solids.

Add the shrimp liquid, rice, chicken stock, sherry, and miso to the pot. Bring to boil. Reduce the heat level to low and cover the pot. Simmer till rice becomes tender, 1/2 hour or so.

Blend the mixture in small-sized batches in the blender. Keep warm.

In a large, non-stick skillet, heat 1 tbsp oil & 1/2 tsp of soup seasoning on med heat. Add the shrimp. Cook for 2 to 4 minutes.

Ladle into individual bowls, & top with the five shrimp. Serve.

10 – Veggie-Chicken Miso Soup

Asian-inspired soup. It adds so much depth to canned chicken broth.

Makes 4 Servings

Cooking + Prep Time: 55 minutes

Ingredients:

- 1 chopped onion, medium
- 6 ounces of de-stemmed, cap-sliced shiitake mushrooms
- 2 thinly sliced stalks of celery
- Kosher salt, as desired
- 2 tbsp of oil, vegetable
- 3 tbsp of miso paste, white
- 2 chicken breasts, boneless, skinless – cut each one in three pieces crosswise
- 4 trimmed, cubed heads of baby Bok choy
- For serving: cilantro leaves, chili paste, lime wedges and/or chopped avocado, as desired
- 6 cups of chicken broth, low-sodium

Instructions:

Heat the oil in a large-sized pot on med-high. Add mushrooms, celery, and onions. Season using kosher salt, as desired. Stir while cooking for 5 to 7 minutes, till vegetables have just started browning and softening.

Add miso and broth to the pot. Bring to boil. Add the chicken, then reduce the heat level. Simmer while covered partially, for 15 to 20 minutes, till chicken has cooked fully through. Meat should show no pink.

Remove the chicken from its broth and shred, then return it to the pot. Add the Bok choy and cover the pot. Cook for 3 to 4 minutes, till Bok choy wilts. Ladle into individual bowls with cilantro, chili paste, lime wedges and/or avocado pieces, as desired. Serve.

11 – Miso Sea Bass

You can eat healthier without compromising the flavors you enjoy. This sea bass is covered with a miso glaze and is easy to prepare, low-calorie dish.

Makes 2 Servings

Cooking + Prep Time: 25 minutes

Ingredients:

- 1 tbsp of miso paste, white
- 1 tbsp + 1 tsp of mirin rice wine
- 1 tsp of honey
- Sea salt, as desired
- 2 fillets of sea bass
- Oil, olive, as needed
- 1 x thumb-sized ginger piece – peel & slice in matchsticks
- 2 tbsp of sweet soy sauce
- 5 & 1/3 ounces of bok choy
- For serving: finely chopped red chili & steamed rice, as desired

Instructions:

Heat your grill for a high heat level.

Mix miso with honey and 1 tsp of mirin. Season bass using sea salt, as desired. Brush miso mixture over the fillets. Lay them on an oiled cookie sheet.

Heat 1 tbsp of mirin, soy sauce, bok choy, and ginger in a small pan till thickened and bubbling.

Place bass under the grill for 2 to 3 minutes, till fish has caramelized edges and is cooked fully through. As desired, drink ginger sauce atop sea bass and serve with red chili and steamed rice.

12 – Tangerine Chicken & Cabbage Salad

This tasty salad is an excellent choice for a wintertime lunch. It also gives you a chance to use the wonderful flavor of the miso-sesame dressing.

Makes 1 Serving

Cooking + Prep Time: 10 minutes

Ingredients:

- 2 tbsp of sliced almonds
- 4 oz. of sliced chicken, pan-roasted, prepared
- 2 cups of Napa cabbage
- 1 peeled, segmented tangerine, with its juice
- 1 thinly sliced scallion
- 2 tbsp of miso-sesame vinaigrette dressing, prepared

Instructions:

Toss the chicken with cabbage, scallion, and tangerine with its juices. Drizzle generously with miso-sesame dressing and top with almonds. Serve.

13 – Miso Avocado Chickpea Toast

Avocado toast seems to be all the rage lately. This recipe pairs a chickpea paste spiked with miso for a more original flavor.

Makes 2 Servings

Cooking + Prep Time: 20 minutes

Ingredients:

- 14 oz. of drained, rinsed chickpeas
- 1 tbsp of miso paste, white
- 1 tsp of sesame oil, toasted
- 1/2 fresh lemon, juice only
- 1 large avocado
- 4 thick, toasted slices of rye or wholemeal bread
- A sprinkle of sesame seeds
- 1 diagonally sliced spring onion

Instructions:

Add chickpeas, sesame oil, miso, and lemon juice in a medium bowl. Crush all these ingredients with a potato masher till you form a paste.

Spoon avocado in a separate bowl. Break up using a fork till it is crushed roughly. Fold avocado through chickpeas and spread on bread. Use sesame seeds and spring onions for sprinkling. Serve.

14 – Spicy Miso & Kimchi Soup

This delicious soup is spicy enough for most people who enjoy Asian food. To give it even more of a kick, you can use additional red chili paste.

Makes 4 Servings

Cooking + Prep Time: 1 & 1/4 hour

Ingredients:

- 1 piece of kombu edible kelp, about 3" x 5"
- 4 cups of filtered water
- 3/4 oz. of bonito flakes
- 4 room temperature eggs, large
- 2/3 cup of prepared kimchi, chopped
- 1/2 cup of 1/2"-cut silken tofu
- 1/4 cup of miso
- 2 tbsp of red chili paste
- To serve: sesame oil and sesame seeds, as desired

Instructions:

Combine 4 cups of water and kombu in the large-sized pot. Allow to set for 25 to 30 minutes, till kombu has softened.

Bring kombu to simmer on med heat. When water begins simmering, remove from the heat. Fish kombu out and discard them.

Add the bonito flakes to the pot. Submerge them by stirring a bit. Return pot to a gentle boil, then reduce the heat to med-low & simmer for 5 to 7 minutes. Remove pot from heat. Allow soup to sit for 12-15 minutes.

Add water to a medium pot. Add eggs and cook in boiling water for 6 minutes. Then transfer to bowl with ice water to halt the cooking process. Allow them to set for 2-3 minutes, till the eggs are cold. Peel the eggs and set them aside.

Strain the soup through a sieve into a medium-sized bowl. Discard the solids and wipe out the pot. Return the soup to the pot.

Add tofu and kimchi to the pot. Bring to a gentle simmer, then remove them from heat. Then submerge a sieve in the liquid. Add miso & chili paste to the sieve. Stir till they liquefy and press them through the strainer till the pastes dissolve.

Ladle the soup into individual bowls. As desired, top them with a drizzle of sesame oil and a scattering of sesame seeds. Halve the eggs and add them. Serve.

15 – Miso-Glazed Ribs

Baby back ribs on the grill are a great summer dish to start with. Glazing them with miso marinade makes them irresistible.

Makes 8 Servings

Cooking + Prep Time: 3 hours & 10 minutes

Ingredients:

- 4 racks of baby back ribs
- 1 quart carton of pineapple juice

For the glaze:

- 4 tbsp of miso paste, white
- 4 tbsp of honey
- 4 tbsp of soy sauce, low sodium

Instructions:

Preheat oven to 350°F. Place ribs with the flesh side facing down on a large-sized roasting tin in one layer. Add pineapple juice poured over ribs. Cover tightly using foil. Cook in 350°F oven for three hours.

Remove ribs from the oven. Scoop 6 & 3/4 fluid ounces of cooking liquid in small pan. Then add all ingredients for the glaze and bring the mixture to simmer. Allow to reduce till glaze is sticky and glossy.

Raise oven heat to 390°F. Turn ribs with the flesh side facing up. Baste them with 1/2 of glaze prepared in step 2. Place ribs in foil-lined pan. Roast in 390°F oven for 30 to 40 minutes. Add additional glaze when halfway done. Serve.

16 – Miso & Pancetta Pasta

Mozzarella cheese, pancetta, and miso may seem to be a strange combination. Once you take your first bite of this dish, you'll see how wonderfully they blend.

Makes 2-4 Servings

Cooking + Prep Time: 50 minutes

Ingredients:

- 3 tbsp of butter, unsalted
- 2 oz. of 1/4"-cubed pancetta
- 1/2 cup of chopped onion
- 2 tbsp of miso
- 1/2 lb. of pasta, uncooked
- 2 tbsp of chopped parsley, + extra as desired
- 1/2 tsp of pepper, black
- 1/2 cup of torn mozzarella cheese, fresh

Instructions:

Melt the butter in a heavy, large skillet. Add the pancetta. Cook for 4 to 5 minutes until the pancetta has rendered and is starting to brown. Add the onions. Cook for 3 to 4 minutes until the pancetta becomes crisp, and onions are soft.

Cook the pasta using directions on the package. Drain and reserve a cup of cooking liquid.

Add miso and reserved pasta cooking liquid to the skillet. Bring mixture to simmer. Add the pasta. Toss constantly while simmering for 1 to 2 minutes till the sauce becomes glossy and has coated the pasta. Add chopped parsley & black pepper. Toss again, coating pasta well. Use mozzarella and extra parsley to garnish, then serve.

17 – Miso Spring Salad

This is a wonderfully easy salad to prepare for the family. You can use any leftover miso dressing in your next grilled tofu or steamed vegetable dish.

Makes 2 Servings

Cooking + Prep Time: 15 minutes

Ingredients:

- 2 cups of spring salad mix, prepared
- 1 sliced avocado
- 1 sliced radish
- 3 sliced cherry tomatoes
- 4 hand-torn mint leaves
- Optional: 1 or 2 radish sprouts with bottoms discarded
- Sweet miso dressing, prepared, as desired

Instructions:

Rinse the salad mix. Allow to completely dry.

Toss the salad mix with avocados, radishes, tomatoes, leaves of mint & radish sprouts (if using) in a large-sized bowl.

Drizzle dressing over salad. Gently toss and serve promptly.

18 – Tahini-Miso Asparagus & Noodles

This is a one-pot recipe that features fresh vegetables & tasty herbs in a popular side dish. The sauce ties all the ingredients together.

Makes 4 Servings

Cooking + Prep Time: 55 minutes

Ingredients:

- 1/3 cup of cashews, chopped
- 1 x peeled & thinly sliced 2-inch piece of ginger
- 1 crushed clove of garlic
- 1/3 cup of soy sauce, low sodium
- 1/4 cup of mirin rice wine
- 1/4 cup of tahini sauce
- 1/4 cup of rice vinegar, unseasoned
- 1 tbsp of white miso, mellow
- 1 x 12-oz. pkg. of drained tofu, firm
- 1 pound of trimmed and 2"-diagonally sliced asparagus
- 12 ounces of lo Mein noodles, fresh
- 3 thinly sliced scallions
- 2 lengthwise-halved, diagonally sliced cucumbers, medium
- 1 & 1/2 cup of mixed, tender torn herbs, like cilantro, basil and/or cilantro
- Kosher salt, as desired

Instructions:

Blend the ginger and garlic with mirin, soy sauce, vinegar, miso, and tahini in a food processor till smooth. Transfer mixture to a large-sized bowl.

Cut the tofu in 1/2-inch strips, then cut in squares. Pat them dry using paper towels. Then add the tofu to a large bowl. Coat by tossing gently.

Cook the asparagus in boiling water in a large pot for 3-4 minutes, till tender and bright green. Transfer to the bowl of iced water so it can cool. Pat it dry. Reserve the asparagus water in the pot.

Bring the reserved water in the pot back up to boil. Cook the noodles using instructions on the package. Drain noodles and rinse them in cold water.

Add noodles, asparagus, cucumbers, scallions & herbs to the tofu bowl. Season with kosher salt, as desired. Toss, coating well.

Ladle the noodles into individual bowls. Top with cashews and serve.

19 – Japanese Miso Rice

If you're bored with plain rice recipes, this Japanese-inspired dish will switch rice up for you. It's a nutritious recipe that features meat and veggies and miso, adding another flavor level.

Makes 4 Servings

Cooking + Prep Time: 1 & 1/2 hour

Ingredients:

- 3 cups of uncooked short-grain Japanese rice
- 1 burdock root
- 1 carrot, medium
- 2 pieces of fish cake (known as chikuwa)

For seasoning:

- 4 tbsp of soy sauce, low sodium
- 3 tbsp of miso
- 2 tbsp of mirin rice wine
- 1 tbsp of sake

Instructions:

Rinse the rice till the water running off is nearly clear. Drain in a fine strainer and shake out excess water. Transfer to the inner bowl of the rice cooker.

Peel burdock root. Half-cut lengthwise, then slice thinly on the diagonal.

In a medium-sized bowl, soak the burdock root for 12-15 minutes, so it won't change color. Replace the water several times. Drain thoroughly.

Peel carrot. Cut lengthwise in half, then thinly slice.

Cut the fish cake into thin pieces.

Combine miso, soy sauce, sake, and mirin in a small bowl. Mix thoroughly. Pour the seasoning blend into the rice cooker. Mix well. Add water to 3 cup marker on the inner bowl.

Add burdock root, fish cake pieces, and carrots atop rice. DON'T mix them with the rice.

Place in a rice cooker. Begin to cook. Use mixed rice option. When the rice has finished cooking, allow it to sit for 10-12 minutes before opening the rice cooker. Then mix all ingredients well and serve.

20 – Miso Chicken Salad

This is a simple salad to make, but the flavors are anything but ordinary. The crunchy lettuce, smoky bacon & zesty miso dressing are enticing and a little addictive.

Makes 4 Servings

Cooking + Prep Time: 55 minutes

Ingredients:

- 4 bacon slices
- 1 & 1/2" piece of peeled, matchstick-cut ginger
- 1 tbsp of soy sauce, low sodium
- 1 tbsp of tahini
- 1 tbsp of miso, white
- 2 tsp of fish sauce, mild
- 3/4 tsp of sesame oil, toasted
- A pinch of granulated sugar
- 4 tbsp of lemon juice, fresh
- 1 yolk from a large egg
- 3/4 cup of oil, vegetable
- Kosher salt, as desired
- Ground pepper, as desired
- 4 cups of skinned chicken meat shredded from small-sized rotisserie
- 1 x 1/2"-thick ribbon-cut leaf lettuce head
- 2 thinly sliced scallions
- To serve: toasted sesame seeds, as desired

Instructions:

Cook the bacon in a medium, dry skillet on med heat. Occasionally turn slices for 5 to 8 minutes, till crisp and brown. Transfer bacon to a plate lined with paper towels and allow it to cool.

Cook the ginger pieces in a small pan with boiling water. Drain and rinse in cold water, then set ginger aside.

In a small bowl, whisk together tahini, soy sauce, fish sauce, miso, sugar, sesame oil & 2 tbsp of fresh lemon juice till you have a smooth mixture.

Whisk the egg yolk with the remainder of lemon juice in a medium bowl, combining well. Stream in 1/2 cup of oil and constantly whisk till the mixture is thick and emulsified. Continue constantly whisking while you gradually add the soy sauce mixture, followed by the last 1/4 cup of oil. Season with kosher salt & ground pepper, as desired.

Toss 1/2 cup of dressing with chicken in a large-sized bowl, coating chicken well. Add the lettuce and a second 1/2 cup of dressing, then toss again. Season with kosher salt & ground pepper, as desired. Crumble-cooked bacon over the top.

Transfer the salad to a serving platter or bowl. Drizzle over the top with 1 tbsp. +/- of dressing. If you have some leftover, that's fine. Top using sesame seeds if using scallions & ginger. Serve.

21 – Miso-Sesame Beans

My family loves green beans, but I wanted a tastier way to serve them. Miso-sesame paste makes a very flavorful sauce, and even the younger ones enjoy it.

Makes 4 Servings

Cooking + Prep Time: 20 minutes

Ingredients:

- 8 oz. of trimmed green beans, fresh
- 2 tbsp of soy sauce, low sodium
- 1/2 tbsp of miso paste, white
- 1/2 tsp of pepper flakes, red
- 4 minced garlic cloves
- 1 tsp of grated ginger root, fresh
- 1 tbsp of toasted sesame seeds

Instructions:

Place beans in steamer insert. Set in a pot over 1" water. Bring to boil, then cover pot and steam beans for 5-6 minutes. Remove from heat. Transfer beans to a serving platter or bowl.

In a small-sized bowl, stir miso paste, soy sauce, ginger, pepper flakes, and garlic together. Pour mixture over beans. Toss, coating well. Sprinkle top with sesame seeds. Serve.

22 – Grilled Miso Potatoes

Boiling the potatoes first before heading out to the grill will help you easily prepare them. The grill will char them a bit and crisp their skins. Adding the melted, seasoned butter makes them special.

Makes 4 Servings

Cooking + Prep Time: 40 minutes

Ingredients:

- 1 & 1/2 pound of potatoes
- 1/4 cup of salt, kosher
- 4 tbsp of butter, unsalted
- 2 tbsp of miso, red
- 1 finely chopped clove of garlic
- 1 tbsp of rice vinegar, seasoned
- 2 tbsp of parsley, chopped
- Pepper, ground, as desired

Instructions:

Prepare your grill for a med-high level of heat.

Bring 1 quart of water, along with potatoes and salt, as desired, to boil in a medium pan on med-high. Reduce the heat level. Simmer for 12 to 14 minutes till tender, then drain. Grill the potatoes and turn them often for 6 to 8 minutes, till charred lightly.

Set a cast-iron, medium skillet on the grill. Place miso and butter in it. Stir while cooking for 2-3 minutes, till the mixture becomes smooth and butter has melted. Remove from the heat. Stir in the vinegar and garlic and season using pepper, as desired.

Transfer the potatoes to the skillet and break some of them into halves. Toss, coating in the miso and butter mixture. Add the parsley. Toss once again and then serve.

23 – Miso-Butter Chicken

I enjoy the thighs as my favorite part of a chicken, and this recipe makes them totally delicious. The miso adds a wonderful flavor that will saturate the chicken, and the honey finishes off the great taste.

Makes 4 Servings

Cooking + Prep Time: 40 minutes

Ingredients:

- 1/4 cup of miso paste, white
- 2 tbsp of softened butter, unsalted
- 1 tbsp of honey, pure
- 1/2 tbsp of vinegar, rice
- 4 chicken thighs – skin-on, bone-in

Instructions:

Preheat oven to 375°

Mix butter, miso paste, rice vinegar, and honey together in a medium bowl. Rub the mixture on thighs, rubbing both over and under the skin. Place chicken thighs in a large-sized roasting pan, spacing them evenly apart.

Bake in 375°F oven for 1/2 hour or so, till juices of chicken are running clear, and meat in the middle has no pink in it. Serve hot.

24 – Maple-Miso Rice & Tofu

The coconut aminos or mana shoyu make this a healthier dish. You can also use low sodium soy sauce, and whichever you use, you'll enjoy the rich, deep flavors.

Makes 4 Servings

Cooking + Prep Time: 1 & 1/2 hour

Ingredients:

- 1 x 14-ounce pkg. of drained & patted dry tofu, firm
- 1" piece of peeled & finely grated ginger
- 1/4 cup + 2 tbsp of coconut aminos, nama shoyu or soy sauce, low sodium
- 2 tbsp of syrup, maple
- 2 tsp of sesame oil, toasted
- 5 tbsp of corn starch
- 2 thinly sliced scallions
- 1 finely grated small clove of garlic
- 1 tbsp of miso, white
- 1 tbsp of rice vinegar, unseasoned
- 1/2 tsp of crushed pepper flakes, red
- For serving: white rice, steamed, as desired
- 2 peeled, matchstick-cut carrots, medium
- 1 cup of cooked edamame, shelled
- 1 tbsp of sesame seeds, toasted
- For serving: cilantro leaves, as desired

Instructions:

Preheat the oven to 400°F. Wrap the tofu in a kitchen towel. Place on rimmed cookie sheet. Add weight to tofu, like a couple of full veggie cans inside a heavy skillet. Allow to set for 10-12 minutes. Unpack the tofu and unwrap it. Transfer to cutting board and dice in 1-inch cubes.

Whisk 1/4 cup of soy sauce, ginger, 1 tsp of sesame oil, and 1 tbsp of syrup together in a large-sized bowl till combined well. Add the tofu and toss gently, coating it. Sprinkle the corn starch on top. Mix till incorporated and allow to sit for 10-12 minutes.

Remove the tofu from its marinade. Spread it onto a cookie sheet lined with baking paper. Bake in 400°F oven for 25 to 30 minutes and turn when half done, till tofu has formed a thin crust and has turned a golden brown.

Whisk the scallions, miso, garlic, pepper flakes, vinegar, 2 tbsp soy sauce, 1 tsp of sesame oil, and 1 tbsp of maple syrup, combining well.

Divide the rice into individual bowls. Top each bowl with carrots, tofu, and edamame. Drizzle using scallion sauce. Use sesame seeds for sprinkling and top with cilantro leaves, if desired. Serve.

25 – Miso Tofu Soup

This soup starts with dashi, the base used in Japan for soup dishes. You can buy various strengths of dashi granules to season this soup to your liking.

Makes 4 Servings

Cooking + Prep Time: 25 minutes

Ingredients:

- 2 tsp of granulated dashi
- 4 cups of water, filtered
- 3 tbsp of miso paste
- 2 x 1/2"- diagonally sliced green onions
- 1 x 8-oz. pkg. of diced tofu, silken

Instructions:

In a medium pan on med-high heat, combine water and dashi granules. Bring to boil. Reduce the heat level to medium, then whisk in miso paste. Add tofu and stir. Separate green onion layers, then add to soup. Gently simmer for 2-3 minutes and serve.

26 – Kimchi Miso Stew

This is a recipe you'll go to again and again. Even new cooks can make it. It's quite delicious and very filling, too.

Makes 4 Servings

Cooking + Prep Time: 40 minutes

Ingredients:

- 1 tbsp of oil, vegetable
- 6 scallions – chop the pale green and white parts and reserve darker green parts
- 4 sliced cloves of garlic
- 1" piece of peeled & finely chopped ginger
- 4 cups of chicken broth, low sodium
- 3 tbsp of hot chili paste
- 3 tbsp of soy sauce, low sodium
- 1 peeled & sliced radish, small
- 1/4 block of firm tofu, silken
- 1/2 cup of kimchi

Instructions:

Heat the oil in a large pan on high heat. Cook the pale green and white scallion parts with ginger and garlic while stirring frequently for 3-4 minutes, till fragrant and softened. Add the broth. Whisk in soy sauce and chili paste. Add the radish. Simmer for 15 to 20 minutes till the radish becomes tender.

Add tofu and kimchi to the pan. Simmer till tofu heats through. Divide stew in individual bowls. Slice reserved tops of scallions, then scatter on top. Serve.

27 – Asian Miso Wafu Burgers

This is Japan's answer to hamburgers. It isn't eaten with a bun, and it's actually more similar to meatloaf. The texture is enhanced by tofu and mushrooms.

Makes 6 Servings

Cooking + Prep Time: 50 minutes

Ingredients:

- 1 x 14-oz. pkg. of tofu, firm
- 1 lb. of beef, ground
- 2 tbsp of miso paste
- 1/2 cup of shiitake mushrooms, sliced
- 1 lightly beaten egg, large
- 1 tsp of salt, kosher
- 1 tsp of pepper, ground
- 1/4 tsp of nutmeg, ground
- 1/4 cup of sweet Japanese wine (mirin)
- 2 tbsp of soy sauce, low sodium
- 1 tsp of garlic paste
- 1/4 tsp of minced ginger root, fresh
- 1 tbsp of oil, vegetable

Instructions:

Place tofu block on a plate. Place a second plate on the top. Set 3-5 lbs. of weight on the top plate. Press tofu in this manner for 9-15 minutes. Drain off accumulated liquid and discard it. Cut tofu in 1/2" cubes.

Combine tofu with ground beef, mushrooms, egg, miso paste, nutmeg, kosher salt & ground pepper. Divide mixture into six balls. Flatten them in patties.

Stir soy sauce, mirin, ginger, and garlic paste in a small-sized bowl. Set the bowl aside.

Heat oil in a large, heavy skillet on med-high. Brown burgers on both sides, 2-3 minutes on each side. Reduce heat level to low. Cover pan. Cook for 4-5 minutes, till juices, are running clear. Drain excess grease and discard.

Pour soy sauce/ginger mixture into the pan. Move pan frequently so the sauce won't burn. Occasionally flip burgers, coating each side with sauce. It will thicken, then make a glaze on your burgers. When the sauce is gone, burgers are ready. Serve.

28 – Turmeric & Sweet Potato Miso Soup

This soup has a rich, smooth taste. The reason is the dashi, the base for most of the delicious Asian soups you enjoy.

Makes 4 Servings

Cooking + Prep Time: 2 & 3/4 hours

Ingredients:

- 1 sweet potato, small
- 4 cups of water, filtered
- 1 x 3" x 5" piece of kombu
- 3/4 oz. of bonito flakes
- 1 x 5 & 1/2 oz can of coconut milk, unsweetened
- 1/4 cup of miso, white
- 1 tbsp of grated turmeric, fresh
- 1 tbsp of lime juice, fresh
- For serving: chili oil, roasted & crushed peanuts &/or coconut flakes, as desired

Instructions:

Preheat the oven to 450°F.

Pierce the sweet potato a few times using a knife or fork. Roast it on a rimmed cookie sheet for 35 to 45 minutes until tender. Allow to cool, scoop out the flesh and discard the skin.

Combine 4 cups of water and kombu in the large-sized pot. Allow to set for 25 to 30 minutes, till the kombu has softened. Bring to simmer on med heat. Once it begins to simmer, remove it from heat promptly. Fish out and discard the kombu.

Add bonito flakes. Stir one time, submerging the flakes. Return to a gentle boil and reduce the heat level. Simmer for 4-6 minutes. Remove the pan from the heat. Allow steeping for 15-20 minutes. Strain dashi through a fine strainer into a medium-sized bowl. Discard the solids and wipe the pot out.

Transfer the dashi to the blender. Add coconut milk, sweet potatoes, turmeric, and miso. Blend till you have a smooth texture. Return dashi to the pot. Bring to a gentle simmer. Remove from the heat & stir in the fresh lime juice.

Divide the soup into individual bowls. Top with peanuts and coconut flakes and drizzle using chili oil. Serve.

29 – Miso Salmon Cakes

Keeping a can or more of salmon in the pantry means you'll always be ready to make these delicious salmon cakes. The sauce is infused with miso, lime juice, and sake, making an ordinary dish extraordinary.

Makes 4 Servings

Cooking + Prep Time: 35 minutes

Ingredients:

- 1 tbsp of oil, vegetable
- 1 tsp of oil, sesame
- 2 chopped garlic cloves
- 1 chopped onion, green
- 1 cup of cream, heavy
- 1 tbsp of miso paste
- 1/4 cup of lime juice, fresh
- 1/4 cup of sake
- 1 & 1/2 cups of breadcrumbs, dry
- 1 x 7-oz. can of drained, flaked salmon
- 1/3 cup of onion, chopped
- 1/4 cup of chopped cilantro, fresh
- 1 egg, large
- 1 tbsp of soy sauce, low sodium
- 1 tbsp of water, filtered
- 2 tbsp of oil, vegetable

Instructions:

Heat oils in a large-sized skillet on med heat. Add garlic and green onion. Cook till tender. Stir in sake and miso paste and blend well. Bring up to simmer. Stir in lime juice and cream. Return to simmer. Cook for 6-8 minutes until the soup thickens. Remove from the heat. Set pan aside.

In a medium-sized bowl, stir breadcrumbs, onions, cilantro, and salmon together. In a small-sized bowl, whisk water, egg, and soy sauce together with a fork. Stir 1/2 of the mixture into the salmon mixture. You can add a bit more if it seems rather dry. It needs to be easily made into patties.

Heat oil in a large-sized skillet on med-high. Form salmon mixture in 4" patties. Fry them till golden brown, 3-4 minutes on each side. Drizzle sauce over them or serve the sauce separately to dip the cakes. Serve.

30 – Grilled Miso-Ginger Asparagus

While the asparagus is at its peak season and very tender, it makes a wonderful dish. The marinade recipe can be used for green bean grilling, too.

Makes 4 Servings

Cooking + Prep Time: 20 minutes

Ingredients:

- 1/4 cup + 2 tbsp of mirin sweet rice wine
- 1/4 cup of miso, white
- 2 tbsp of seasoned vinegar, rice wine
- 2 tsp of grated & peeled ginger, fresh
- 2 bunches of trimmed asparagus
- For serving: toasted sesame seeds, fresh lime wedges and/or thin-sliced scallions, as desired

Instructions:

Prepare your grill for a high heat level.

Whisk miso, mirin, ginger, and vinegar in a small-sized bowl. Place the asparagus in a small casserole dish. Pour the miso mixture on top. Toss, coating well.

Turn the asparagus occasionally while grilling for 4 to 6 minutes, till it is tender-crisp, and all sides are charred. Transfer asparagus to a serving platter. Squeeze lime juice on top, if desired. Add sesame seeds and scallions, as desired. Serve.

Conclusion

This miso cookbook has shown you...

How to use different ingredients to affect unique tastes in many Asian-based dishes

How can you include miso recipes in your home repertoire?

You can...

Make vegetable miso soups, with choices like Bok choy and eggplant. They are just as tasty as they sound.

Cook miso soups with meat, which are widely served in Asia. Whether you choose chicken, ribs, or other meat, the dishes will surely be a hit.

Enjoy making the delectable seafood miso dishes, including salmon, shrimp, and clams. Fish is a mainstay in recipes year-round, and there are SO many ways to make it great.

Make miso soups with other vegetables, like asparagus and green beans. There is something about them that makes them more filling.

Make miso soup with tofu for a different flavor and texture. It's tasty and tempting for your dinner guests.

Share these special recipes with your friends!

Author Biography

Growing up with parents from different cultures, who had different traditions gave Rose Rivera a chance to taste the cuisines of two different worlds. Her first step in the cooking career was when she started combining ingredients from dishes from different cuisines.

At that time, she ended up with creations that she couldn't believe. Her mom and dad, and everyone else in the family was surprised about her cooking skills, which gave her even more strength and determination to continue cooking and pursue school and career.

Now Rose is trying to reach everyone in the world through food. Whether it's about classic or innovating recipes, people who got her cookbooks never had a hard time following her instructions. It made things better for them, even for those who weren't spending a lot of time in the kitchen.

Inspired by culture and tradition Rose reached the stars. But she is not stopping anytime soon. She believes that there is no end in cooking and she will continue to cook and create recipes as long as she could.

She says, "Don't be afraid to mix it up sometimes, you never know what you will end up with, maybe your own signature dish. Well, that's it all started for me."

So, you defiantly won't be disappointed with her cookbooks. Once you try out the recipes from one of her books you would like to see all of them.

Thank You!

thank you

This won't be my last book, in fact, there are many books coming soon. So, thank you for getting this book because you will see with your own eyes, smell, and taste that my recipes are worth buying. Your cooking skills will get better and you will have different dishes to serve daily.

I appreciate you for choosing my work, I know you won't be disappointed. Now it's time to try out the recipes and share your experience. Leave feedback so that not only others will know about it but also, I'll be able to become even better in my work, every feedback is welcomed.

Thank you once more for choosing my book

Have an amazing day

Rose Rivera

Printed in Great Britain
by Amazon

10139277R00047